First published in Great Britain 2020 by Red Shed, part of Farshore

An imprint of HarperCollins*Publishers*
1 London Bridge Street, London SE1 9GF
www.farshore.co.uk

HarperCollins*Publishers*
1st Floor, Watermarque Building, Ringsend Road, Dublin 4, Ireland

Text copyright © HarperCollins*Publishers* Limited 2020
Illustrations copyright © Jez Tuya 2020

Written by Chris Oxlade.

The illustrator has asserted his moral rights.

ISBN 978 1 4052 9725 7
Printed in the UK by Pureprint a CarbonNeutral® company
002

A CIP catalogue record for this title is available from the British Library.

Stay safe online Farshore is not responsible for content hosted by third parties.

Farshore takes its responsibility to the planet and its inhabitants very seriously.
We aim to use papers from well-managed forests run by responsible suppliers.

FIND, FIX, GO!

Chris Oxlade

RED SHED

Jez Tuya

Vehicles come in all shapes and sizes, and do lots of important jobs. A fire engine hurries to put out fires. A digger digs big holes in the ground, and cars take you where you need to go.

But how do they all work, and what is going on inside? Take a look and find out.

Uh-oh! Each vehicle has something broken! Can you find the problem? If you need help, turn to the back of the book for answers.

FIND IT. The chain has fallen off this bicycle!

It's time to
FIX IT.

Now you can
GO!

Here is Bob Cat's car. It's a modern car, called a **hybrid**.

It has an electric motor and an engine to make it go.

A battery makes the electric motor go. If it runs out of electricity, the engine takes over. The engine runs on petrol, which is stored in the fuel tank.

Boot

Can you spot these parts?

Battery	Electric motor	Engine	Fuel tank	Radiator

    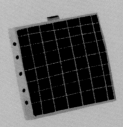

The battery makes the electric motor work.

The electric motor turns the car's wheels.

The engine uses fuel to turn the wheels if the battery runs out.

The fuel tank stores petrol for the engine.

The radiator stops the engine from getting too hot.

Windscreen

FIND, FIX, GO!

Can you see what's wrong with Bob Cat's car? What does he need to do to fix the problem?

Wheel

The car has four wheels which allow it to move along.

Tyre

Tyres make the journey less bumpy. They grip the road so the car doesn't skid.

Brakes

Brakes slow the car down. The brake discs are made of metal.

Suspension

Suspension makes the car travel smoothly over bumps.

Wing mirror

The wing mirror lets Bob Cat see the road behind him when he drives along.

A **motorcyle** is a super speedy two-wheeled machine. Henry Hippo loves his motorcycle!

The big engine and the smooth shape help it to go really fast.

GARAGE

EXHAUST REPAIR KIT SALE!

PETROL

The petrol tank stores fuel.

Headlight

Kickstand

Can you spot these parts?

Engine

The engine needs petrol to make the motorcycle go.

Chain

The engine drives the chain, which turns the back wheel.

Exhaust

Waste gas from the engine flows out through the exhaust pipe.

Handlebars

The rider steers the motorcycle using the handlebars.

Front forks

The front forks let the wheels go up and down gently over bumps.

Brake

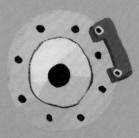

Brake discs on the wheels slow the motorcycle down and make it stop.

FIND, FIX, GO!

Henry can't ride his motorcycle because a part is broken.

Can you spot something in the garage shop window that will fix the problem?

This is a **digger**. It's a big machine for digging holes in the ground.

Bella Beaver is in charge! Her digger has a long arm with a big bucket on the end for scooping up soil.

The levers move the arm.

The driver in the cab pulls the levers.

A digger trundles along on metal tracks. The tracks stop the digger from sinking into sticky mud on a building site.

FIND, FIX, GO!

Uh-oh! The digger won't move. What has come loose, and what can Bella do to get it rolling again?

Can you spot these parts?

Driver controls

The driver pulls and pushes levers to move parts of the digger.

Engine

The engine powers the tracks, the arm and the bucket.

Bucket

A large metal bucket bites into the soil with sharp teeth.

Hydraulic cylinder

Cylinders are like big muscles that move the arm and bucket.

Track

Tracks made of metal plates bolted together move the digger around the site.

Sprocket

Sprockets have sharp teeth that grip the tracks and make them turn.

This truck is a **concrete mixer**. It mixes cement, gravel, sand and water to make concrete. Rory Raccoon is driving it.

The huge drum spins slowly round and round, mixing the concrete on the way to the building site.

A wheelbarrow is waiting to catch the concrete.

At the building site Rory unfolds the delivery chute. Then the drum spins backwards to push out the concrete.

Water in the water tank keeps concrete wet.

FIND, FIX, GO!

Oh, no! There's a loud clanging noise, but where is it coming from? What can Rory and the team do to fix it?

Can you spot these parts?

Engine

The engine drives the truck and makes the mixing drum spin.

Delivery controls

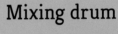

These levers and buttons control the mixing drum.

Feeder hopper

Cement, sand, gravel and water are poured into this container.

Mixing drum

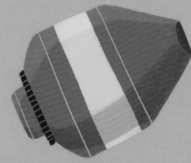

The drum is a big container. This is where the concrete gets mixed up.

Drum blades

As the drum spins slowly, the blades inside mix the concrete.

Delivery chute

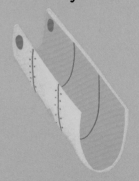

Sloppy, wet concrete slides down the delivery chute.

A **fire engine** rushes to a fire with its lights flashing and its sirens blaring. On board is all the kit firefighters need to put out a fire.

Carla Crocodile connects a hose and sprays water on the fire.

Can you spot these parts?

Emergency light	Axe	Water tank	Water pump	Hose
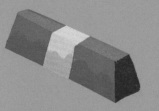			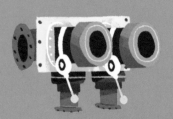	
Flashing lights warn people that a fire truck is coming.	This tool is for breaking through doors and walls.	The on-board water tank carries water for putting out fires.	A powerful pump pushes water along the hoses.	Hoses carry water from the tank towards the fire.

Sirens

FIND, FIX, GO!
Daphne Duck is confused – where is the water? What can she do to fix the problem?

Water nozzle	Ladder	Radio	Portable water pump	Shovel
The nozzle at the nd of the hose aims water at the fire.	Ladders are for climbing up to windows.	Firefighters use the radio to call for extra help.	This pump helps to clear up flood water.	Firefighters use a shovel to clear up after a fire.

This **train** is at the station! It has a locomotive and carriages. The locomotive has a huge diesel engine. It pulls the carriages with passengers inside.

Dougie Dog is in charge of repairs.

Can you spot these parts?

Light	Battery box	Fuel tank	Diesel engine

White lights at the front of the train light up the track ahead.	The battery stores electricity to start the engine.	The tank contains diesel, which is the fuel that makes the engine go.	This big powerful engine turns the wheels and pushes the train along.

STATION

FIND, FIX, GO!
Something is broken and the train is held up! Can you see the problem? What can Dougie Dog do to fix it?

Driver controls

he driver pushes the lever
o speed up, and pulls it to
slow the train down.

Coupling

A coupling is the part that
connects the locomotive
to a carriage.

Wheel

A train wheel is made
from solid metal. Trains
have lots of wheels.

Toilet

The carriage has a
toilet – for passengers
who need to go!

A **motorboat** is a very fast boat that skims over the water at top speed! Cooper Cat loves to dive off the side into the sea.

The boat is pushed along by an engine. The engine turns a propeller at the back of the boat. The propeller pushes on the water and the boat zooms forwards.

The body of the boat is called the hull.

Radio

The anchor grips the sea bed and stops the boat moving.

DIVE TOURS

FIND, FIX, GO!
Oh-oh! The boat has stopped. Cooper has dived in the water to investigate! What should she do?

Can you spot these parts?

Fuel tank

The fuel tank is where fuel for the engine is stored.

Engine

The engine turns the boat's propeller.

Propeller

The propeller spins around and pushes the boat forwards.

Wheel

The driver turns the wheel, which turns the propeller and steers the boat.

Throttle

This lever controls the engine. It makes the boat speed up or slow down.

Life buoy
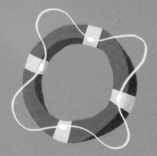

If someone falls overboard, this helps them stay afloat until they can be rescued.

Percy Penguin is a pilot and he flies an **aeroplane.** An aeroplane is a flying machine with two wings that lift it into the air.

The plane has a propeller that pushes it forwards. The pilot has controls to move flaps on the plane and steer it through the air.

Wing

Can you spot these parts?

Seat

The pilot sits in a comfortable seat in the cockpit.

Throttle

The pilot pulls or pushes the throttle to control the speed.

Propeller

The propeller pulls the plane through the air.

Engine

The powerful engine spins the propeller round.

Air traffic control tower

Cockpit

FIND, FIX, GO!

Percy is grounded! All the ice is stopping him from taking off. What should he do?

Fuel tank

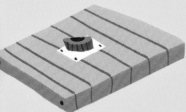

The fuel tank is full of fuel for the engine.

Rudder

The rudder makes the plane turn right or left.

Aileron

Two ailerons make the plane tip to one side or the other.

Landing gear

The landing gear comes out when the plane is on the ground or lands. It lets the plane roll along the ground.

A **helicopter** is a flying machine and Frankie Fox loves to fly!

Long, thin blades like wings lift the helicopter upwards and into the air.

Main rotor

A powerful engine turns the main rotor. It goes so fast that the blades become a blur.

Cockpit

FIND, FIX, GO!

Frankie Fox is in a hurry but there's something wrong with her helicopter. How will she fix it and take off?

Blade

Can you spot these parts?

Skids

The helicopter sits on its skids when it is on the ground.

Control stick

Moving the control stick makes the helicopter change direction.

Engine

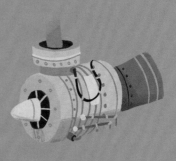

The engine turns the main rotor and the tail rotor.

Tail rotor

The tail rotor stops the helicopter from spinning round.

Tail fin

This fin helps to steer the helicopter as it zooms along.

Stabiliser fins

These fins stick out sideways. They keep the helicopter level.

A spacecraft is a rocket-fuelled machine that whizzes into space. It carries astronauts to a space station high above the Earth.

There is no air in space, but the spacecraft is filled with air for the astronauts to breathe.

Monty Monkey is outside the spacecraft! He is wearing a spacesuit that is attached to the spacecraft with a tether.

Control panel

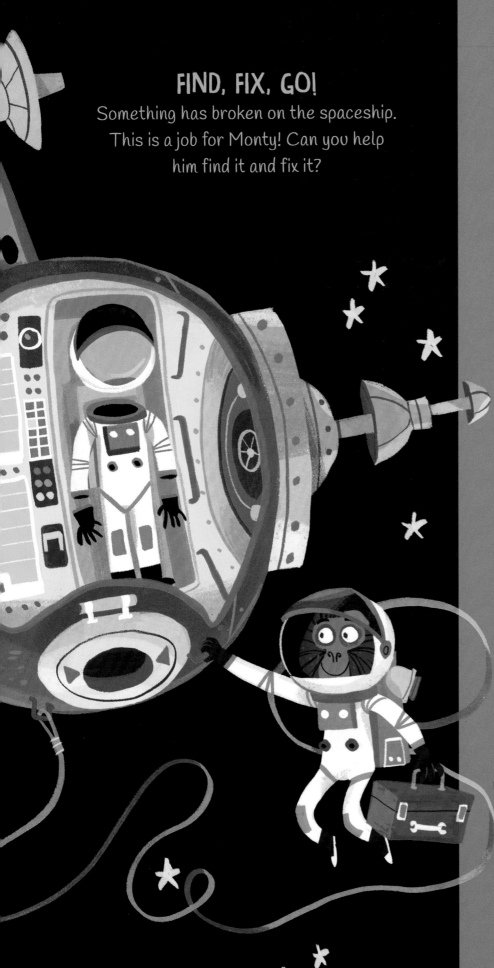

FIND, FIX, GO!

Something has broken on the spaceship. This is a job for Monty! Can you help him find it and fix it?

Can you spot these parts?

End hatch

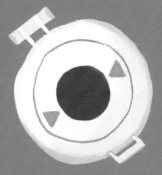

The astronauts climb in and out through the end hatch.

Radio aerial

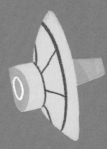

This aerial sends radio signals back down to Earth.

Side thruster

The thruster makes the spacecraft spin round.

Solar panel

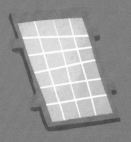

Solar panels use sunlight to make electricity for the spacecraft.

Docking mechanism

This is needed when the spaceship connects to a space station.

Main engine

The powerful main engine pushes the spacecraft forwards.

Did you solve all the breakdown problems?

Check the answers and find out if you worked out how to fix the vehicles on every page!

Car Bob Cat has a flat tyre. He can use the jack to lift the wheel and swap it for the spare wheel, which is in the boot.

Motorcycle The exhaust pipe is cracked. Henry Hippo needs to buy an exhaust repair kit from the garage shop.

Digger The bolts have fallen out of the tracks. Bella Beaver can screw the bolts back in so the tracks fit together again.

Concrete mixer Rory Raccoon will have to stop the drum so that the team can pull out the spade.

Fire engine The hose has come off the water pump, so Daphne Duck needs to attach it again.

Train There is a broken wheel. Dougie Dog has a spare wheel in his wheelbarrow so he can replace the broken one.

Motorboat The propeller is tangled up with seaweed. Cooper Cat can use the knife on the boat to cut it away.

Aeroplane The plane is icy. Percy Penguin can spray de-icer from the de-icing machine on to the plane to melt the ice.

Helicopter One of the rotor blades is bent. Frankie Fox needs to attach the spare blade, which is on the ground.

Spacecraft Some wires on the solar panel have come out. Monty Monkey needs to fix the wires.